ELECTROLYTE

by James Meteyard

Music and Lyrics by

Maimuna Memon

samuelfrench.co.uk

For Amateur Production Enquiries

United Kingdom and World
excluding North America

plays@samuelfrench.co.uk

020 7255 4302/01

Each title is subject to availability from Samuel French, depending upon country of performance.

THINKING ABOUT PERFORMING A SHOW?

There are thousands of plays and musicals available to perform from Samuel French right now, and applying for a licence is easier and more affordable than you might think

From classic plays to brand new musicals, from monologues to epic dramas, there are shows for everyone.

Plays and musicals are protected by copyright law, so if you want to perform them, the first thing you'll need is a licence. This simple process helps support the playwright by ensuring they get paid for their work and means that you'll have the documents you need to stage the show in public.

Not all our shows are available to perform all the time, so it's important to check and apply for a licence before you start rehearsals or commit to doing the show.

LEARN MORE & FIND THOUSANDS OF SHOWS

Browse our full range of plays and musicals, and find out more about how to license a show

www.samuelfrench.co.uk/perform

Talk to the friendly experts in our Licensing team for advice on choosing a show and help with licensing

plays@samuelfrench.co.uk   020 7387 9373

Acting Editions

BORN TO PERFORM

Playscripts designed from the ground up to work the way you do in rehearsal, performance and study

---

Larger, clearer text for easier reading

Wider margins for notes

Performance features such as character and props lists, sound and lighting cues, and more

---

+ CHOOSE A SIZE AND STYLE TO SUIT YOU

  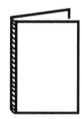

STANDARD EDITION

Our regular paperback book at our regular size

SPIRAL-BOUND EDITION

The same size as the Standard Edition, but with a sturdy, easy-to-fold, easy-to-hold spiral-bound spine

LARGE EDITION

A4 size and spiral bound, with larger text and a blank page for notes opposite every page of text – perfect for technical and directing use

---

LEARN MORE | **samuelfrench.co.uk/actingeditions**

MUSIC USE NOTE

The music parts for this title are available on hire to licensed productions from Samuel French. Fees and conditions of this hire are quoted on application.

Sample materials are available on request for perusal prior to application.

IMPORTANT BILLING AND CREDIT REQUIREMENTS

If you have obtained performance rights to this title, please refer to your licensing agreement for important billing and credit requirements.

Electrolyte previewed at Theatre503 on 23 and 24 July 2018. It then ran from 1–27 August at QueenDome, Pleasance at The Edinburgh Fringe Festival 2018.

It then played at 32 venues across the UK and Ireland during the spring/summer 2019 with the following cast and creative team:

CAST

JESSIE	Olivia Sweeney
PAUL	Ben Simon
DONNA	Megan Ashley
RALPH	Chris Georgiou
ALLIE	Maimuna Memon
JIM	James Meteyard

Writer & Associate Director	James Meteyard
Music & Lyrics	Maimuna Memon
Director	Donnacadh O'Briain
Producer	Joseph Dawson
Costume	Hannah Hodge
Lighting	Timothy Kelly
Sound Engineer	Piotr Dubrowski

Electrolyte was developed collaboratively by the company.

CAST AND CREATIVES

OLIVIA SWEENEY - JESSIE

Olivia's work in theatre includes: *Macbeth* for The National Theatre; *Electrolyte* and *After Party* for Wildcard; *The Secret Garden* for Theatre by the Lake Keswick; *Mighty Atoms* for Hull Truck; *The Maids* for Square Peg; *Hoax: My Lonely Heart* and *Come Closer* at The Royal Exchange; *My Brother's Country* for Routes North; *That Dead Girl* at The Arcola; *Noura* at Theatre503; *In My Bed* for Milk and Two Sugars and *Black and White* and *As You Like It* for The National Youth Theatre's REP Company.
TV includes: *Coronation Street, Doctors* and *Ordinary Lies*.
Film includes: *Aux, 7.2, Three in a Bed* and *Celluloid*.
Radio includes: *Stone*.
Olivia was involved in the development of *Electrolyte* from an early stage after working with James on his first play, *After Party*.

BEN SIMON - PAUL

Ben is a graduate of The Oxford School of Drama. Credits include: *Catch of the Day* (Red Fox Theatre/The Tron); *Henry V* (Rose Playhouse); *Mr Pottle's Revenge* (Karman Theatre/The Vaults); *Attempts on Her Life* (Oxford School of Drama/Soho Theatre) and *If and When* (Oxford School of Drama/Soho Theatre). He worked as Musical Director and musician on *Lilith: Confessions of a Demon Goddess*; part of the Damsel Develops Festival at the Bunker Theatre (Damsel Productions/The Bunker). Ben is a founding member of Red Fox Theatre whose first production, *Catch of the Day*, premiered at the Edinburgh Fringe Festival in 2018 and was nominated for the Best Musical Award.
Ben began working on *Electrolyte* in November 2017 and having been involved throughout the journey is delighted to be back on board for

the tour. He would like to thank everyone at Wildcard Theatre for what has been a wonderful experience.

MEGAN ASHLEY - DONNA

Megan is a graduate of Guildford School of Acting with a BA (Hons) in Musical Theatre. Theatre credits include: Gerda in *The Snow Queen* (Under The Bridge Theatre); Witch, Lady Macduff and Musician in *Macbeth* (International Tour, S4K International); Snow White in *Snow White and the Seven Dwarfs* (The Stiwt); Vocalist in *Olivier Awards: In Concert* (BBC Radio 2, Royal Festival Hall); Soloist in *Fabulous 50* (The Yvonne Arnaud); General Cartwright in *Guys and Dolls* (The Yvonne Arnaud); Lotte Lenya in *Speak Low* (World Premier, PATS Centre); Miss Dorothy in *Thoroughly Modern Millie* (Ivy Arts Centre); Soloist in *Here's Where I Stand: GSA Singers* (Electric Theatre); Precious McGuire in *Steel Pier* (Ivy Arts Centre).

Workshops include: *Soul Music* (Craig Adams) and *Lia's Guide to Winning the Lottery* (Perfect Pitch).

Megan came on board with *Electrolyte* in July 2018, originating the part of Donna at the Edinburgh Fringe Festival. She is very excited to be back again with Wildcard Theatre for the 2019 UK tour and is very grateful to be part of a show that conveys such a beautiful message about friendship and support when it comes to mental health.

CHRIS GEORGIOU - RALPH

Chris is an actor, drummer, and music producer. He trained at Italia Conti Academy of Theatre Arts and Drama Centre London. When he's not acting, he's drumming, producing songs, and working on his ethical clothing brand 'Brothers Of Mother Earth'.

MAIMUNA MEMON - ALLIE TOUCH

Maimuna is a Lancashire-born, British-Pakistani singer-songwriter, musician and actress, who trained at The Oxford School of Drama. Theatre credits include: *Into The Woods* (The Royal Exchange); *Buskers Opera* (Park Theatre); *Lazarus* (Kings Cross Theatre); *Winnie and Wilbur* (Birmingham Rep); *Jesus Christ Superstar* (Regent's Park Open Air Theatre); *The Assasination of Katie Hopkins* (Theatr Clwyd); *Standing at The Sky's Edge* (Sheffield Crucible) and *Hobson's Choice* (Royal Exchange).

Television credits include: *Doctors* and *Unforgotten* series 3. Musical Director credits include: *Macbeth* (The Watermill Theatre); *A Midsummer Night's Dream* (The Brockley Jack Theatre) and *Electrolyte*. Music has always been a huge part of her life, and so she continued to write and compose throughout her training and alongside her professional acting career. Although she has written music for ten years, *Electrolyte* is her first professional composition for theatre. Maimuna is very passionate about diversifying the world of songwriting and composition and wants to encourage composers and creatives from every background to step into the light and shine.

JAMES METEYARD - JIM

James Meteyard is an actor, writer and director. He trained at The Oxford School of Drama.

As an actor his theatre credits include: *Electrolyte* (Pleasance, Edinburgh Fringe/UK Tour); *Coriolanus* (Rose Theatre, Bankside); *After Party* (The Pleasance, Islington); *Troilus and Cressida* (Edinburgh Fringe) and *Macbeth* (Broadway Theatre).

His Feature Film credits include: *Moths* (Dir. Sam Fenton).
As a director his credits include: *After Party* (Union theatre), *A Midsummer Night's Dream* (Jack Studio Theatre).
Associate Director: *Electrolyte* (UK Tour); *Coriolanus* (Rose Bankside); *Troilus and Cressida* (Rose Bankside/Edinburgh Fringe).
As a writer his credits include: *Electrolyte* (Pleasance/UK Tour), *After Party* (Pleasance).
James is Joint-Artistic Director of Wildcard.

CREATIVES

DONNACADH O'BRIAIN - DIRECTOR

Donnacadh is a new writing specialist, whose productions have played at The Royal Shakespeare Company, in the West End, and internationally. His acclaimed production of *Rotterdam* by Jon Brittain won the 2017 Olivier Award for Outstanding Achievement in an Affiliate Theatre. In summer 2019, he has both *Electrolyte* and *Rotterdam* on major UK tours.
Recent productions include: *Loam* by Bea Roberts (RWCMD, Gate Theatre); *Rejoicing at Her Wondrous Vulva, the Young Woman Applauded Herself* by Bella Heesom (Ovalhouse); *Mother Christmas* by David Lewis (Hampstead Theatre Downstairs) and *Lads* by Jon Brittain (LAMDA). He has several new shows in development, and later this year he will direct a new play on border control he has co-written with Amy Ng (*Ice & Fire*, touring).
Favourite productions include: *Always Orange* by Fraser Grace for the RSC, which reopened The Other Place Theatre; *My World Has Exploded a Little Bit* developed with and written by Bella Heesom; *The Easter Rising and Thereafter*, devised with Sir Christopher Bland for the centenary of the uprising; *PEEP* at Edinburgh and Latitude festivals featuring new plays writers including Leo Butler, Pamela Carter, Luke Barnes, Kay Adshead and Kefi Chadwick; a major Irish production of *King Lear* staring the late great Gerard Murphy; and as an Assistant director to Michael Boyd, the RSC's multi-award-winning *Histories Cycle* (the *Guardian*'s 'Production of the Decade').

TIMOTHY KELLY - LIGHTING DESIGNER

Timothy Kelly is an inter-disciplinary theatre creative, with experience across lighting and projection design, performance and directing. He likes bold theatre that plays with form. He is interested the intersection of technology and accessibility in theatre and has built a creative captioning engine for shows with d/Deaf and hearing casts, and built an app to help enable people with severe learning disabilities to operate lighting and sound.

Credits include: *The Noises* (Lighting Designer, Old Red Lion); *Orangutan* (Lighting Designer & Production Manager, VAULT); *Jade City* (Lighting & Set, VAULT); *17* (Projection Designer, VAULT); *The Trench* (Associate Lighting Designer, Southwark Playhouse & UK Tour); *Sirens* (Lighting & Projection Designer, UK Tour & Edinburgh Fringe); *Mr Brightside* (Lighting Designer, Brighton Fringe, Greenwich Theatre & Matthew's Yard).

LUKE W ROBSON - SET DESIGNER

Designs include: *Tokyo Rose* (Burnt Lemon – New Diorama, Underbelly); *Electrolyte* (Wildcard Theatre – UK Tour); *My Kind of Michael* (UK Tour); *2030* (Crowded Room); *Circa* (Old Red Lion); *Work Bitch* and *Finding Fassbender* (VAULTS Festival); *Handel Messiah* (Porchester Hall); *It's True, It's True, It's True* (New Diorama Theatre, Underbelly); *Velvet* (Pleasance); *Sapho and Phao* (RSC); *Small Town Politics* (Sky Arts); *Unspoken* (Theatre Royal); *Live Lab Elevator, The Terminal Velocity of Snowflakes* (Live Theatre); *Madam Butterfly* (King's Head Theatre); *Fans* (Tour); *Odd Shaped Balls* (Old Red Lion – OFFIE Nominee – Best Set Design); *The Nether, Journey's End* and *The Pillowman* (Northern Stage).

Art projects include: a Digital Artist Residency with OVADA, *Here's To Thee, Old Apple Tree* (RSC); *The Cave* (Queens Hall Digital, Great North Museum, Hoxton Arches) and *Electric Sheep* (Channel 4, Random Acts). In 2018 Luke was the recipient of the Leverhulme Trust Bursary as Assistant Designer at the Royal Shakespeare Company, finalist for Best Newcomer at The Journal Culture Awards and shortlisted for the Old Vic 12.

PIOTR DUBROWSKI - SOUND DESIGNER/ENGINEER

Piotr has worked as a Technical Operator during *Electrolyte*'s first run at the Edinburgh Fringe Festival and he now joins the team as a Sound Engineer for their first UK and Ireland tour. He is a graduate of Glasgow Caledonian University with a BSc (Hons) in Audio Technology with Multimedia and he also holds an HND in Sound Production from Edinburgh's Jewel & Esk College.

Piotr has worked in live events industry for a number of years and has also produced music and created sound design for various clients and art exhibitions. As a true sound enthusiast with love for music and keen interest in technology, Piotr finds *Electrolyte* as a perfect platform for merging his passions and showcasing his skills.

JOSEPH DAWSON - PRODUCER

Joseph Dawson's producing credits include: *Electrolyte* (National Tour); *17* (VAULT Festival 2019); *Electrolyte* (Edinburgh Festival Fringe 2018); *The Cat's Mother* (VAULT Festival 2018 / Edinburgh Festival Fringe 2018); *After Party* (Pleasance Theatre) and *A Midsummer Night's Dream* (Broadway Theatre & Brockley Jack Studio Theatre). Joseph is a founding member of Wildcard and manages the company on a day-to-day basis.

Joseph is also a proud member of ITC and an alumni of Stage One. He fell into producing completely by accident and has fallen in love with it. He enjoys bringing people together to tell interesting and emotive stories.

AUTHOR'S NOTE

Jessie should be played by one performer.

The text should be more or less entirely underscored by live music that should be performed by actor-musicians who also play the other characters. The production should be presented as if it were a gig.

The characters of **Allie** and **Mum** should be played by the same performer.

Spoken text and rap lyrics are written on the left and song lyrics are written on the right.

...   represents a search for a thought or a sense of space at the end of a line.

Beat   represents a change in feeling, thought or action.

–   at the end of a line represents an interruption.

HOW ELECTROLYTE WAS CONCEIVED AND MADE

For about six or seven years now I've wanted to create a piece of gig theatre, first attempting it five years ago using beatboxing and live looping. However, this was quickly abandoned as the complexities of the form started to emerge.

Since then I've been inspired by a number of companies and productions including the work of Middle Child, Paines Plough and Nabakov. From these productions I started to see patterns of when I thought gig theatre worked amazingly well. It was the moments where I was swept away from a theatre venue and into the world of the story, transported by music that I couldn't help but move to – both physically and emotionally – and yet somehow, at the same time I was completely there, in those theatres, enjoying and totally present to a celebration of musical brilliance, that placed the musicians at the forefront of the experience in a way that only a gig really does.

I knew I wanted to explore this form and at the time a close family member was coming through a mental health crisis. During this time, I'd researched shocking statistics relating to mental health problems in this country. This made me realise that there are millions of people who may not have the same support network that my family member had or perhaps don't realise that they are that support for someone in their life until it's too late. I wanted to write a piece that shared a very real story that could happen to any of us, with the hope it might encourage people to be aware of how their actions could impact those around them and inspire people to reach out and be there for one another when times get tough.

I started writing *Electrolyte* in April 2017 for a phenomenal actress and human, Olivia Sweeney, who has helped shape this piece right from the beginning in an extraordinary way. By September I had a first draft ready and I knew of only one person who could bring the music to life. The exceptionally talented Maimuna Memon, an actor-musician I trained at The Oxford School of Drama with. I knew she was keen to compose for theatre and when I approached her she leapt on the idea with incredible passion and enthusiasm.

Following this we completed a week of R&D at The Watermill Theatre and another week of R&D at Theatr Clwyd where we were joined by Ben Simon & Chris Georgiou. It was here that we created the bulk of the score together, working off one another and developing the piece through play, trial and error! Following this we rehearsed for four weeks in London at Clapham Omnibus & Ovalhouse where Megan Ashley joined us to complete the cast and Donnacadh O'Briain joined as director. It was here we finished the development of the score and did most of the redrafts on the script. Donnacadh pushed to strip back the story so it rips along with the pace of a live gig, sweeping the audience up. We developed a style of playing the piece which feels very 'knockabout' but underneath the pretence is an extremely tight production that took weeks of rehearsal to finesse.

After over a year of development we finally opened the show at the Edinburgh Fringe 2018! During the process of taking such a technically heavy show up to the Fringe I'd almost forgotten why I'd written it. So it was an extraordinary experience when audiences members started coming straight up to us after every show had finished to share their experiences with mental health problems. This was incredibly powerful as it goes to show not only how common mental health problems are but also how important it is to encourage conversation around the subject. We also received some lovely reviews and were awarded a number awards, including The Mental Health Fringe Award. This was a real honour as I was nervous about writing about mental health due to it being a very sensitive subject.

Ultimately the piece champions togetherness as a way of combating poor mental health and Edinburgh showed us that this is a story that should be told further. So following Edinburgh we embarked on a ten week tour, playing at thirty two venues, across the UK and Ireland. We combined this with an outreach programme made up of workshops and discussions centred around mental health and creativity. During this time Robyn Sinclair joined us, taking on the role of Allie Touch.

We're now extremely excited to be bringing this show back to the Edinburgh Fringe Festival for August 2019. It feels like it's where it all began for us and we're over the moon to be playing there again.

This has been an incredible journey and it wouldn't have been possible without the help of so many wonderful people and organisations. Thank you to everyone who has supported *Electrolyte* and to those who will support it's future. I hope you enjoy it.

James Meteyard, July 2019

WITH SPECIAL THANKS TO:

To Liv, Ben and Chris for believing in this from the beginning, Joey for helping to make it all happen, Hattie for her wonderful support, Paul Hart & Abigail Pickard Price at The Watermill Theatre for all they have done, all the team at Theatr Clwyd, Steven, Charlie and all of the team at Samuel French, Fiona, James and Oli at Les Enfants Terribles, Jack Shanks for his videography, David at St Gabriel's Hall for being so generous, James Spencer for his support with MC lyrics, The Oxford School of Drama, Ovalhouse, Omnibus Theatre, Unity Theatre Trust, ETT, John and Ria at The North Wall, Mark Makin and all at house theatre, the Wildcard family for their constant inspiration, love and talent, everyone who supported our crowdfunding campaign and everyone who has helped us workshop the piece.

James would like to thank:

My dad for being so supportive and also my unofficial dramaturg, my sister for being a constant source of light in my life, my mum for all of her love and all that she has taught me, Liv for all of her love and brilliance, my friends for all of their support and inspiration, and to the whole cast and creative team for their incredible work.

Maimuna would like to thank:

Richard for all your love, support and creativity, Mum for injecting music into me since birth, Dad for inspiring me with your insatiable drive and determination, Adil, Itrat and Yusuf for being incredible brothers, James, Jess, Aileen and George at Hatton McEwan Penford for always believing in me, every friend who's ever come to support me at my gigs over the years, and to James, for this exceptional story and for taking me on this wonderful adventure.

For my mum, who made me who I am.

May you rest with the angels.

CHARACTER

JESSIE – A girl from Leeds, late twenties

PAUL – Donna's boyfriend and a friend of Jessie's

DONNA – Jessie's best friend

RALPH – One of Jessie's oldest and closest friends

ALLIE – A singer/songwriter from Leeds

MUM – Jessie's Mother

JIM – A lad from London

MAN – An abusive partner of Jessie's Mum

STRANGER – A stranger in the street

POLICE OFFICER – An emergency call operator

MC – A host at a warehouse party in London

A gig in Leeds. Nothing is on stage except for the performers and their instruments.

JESSIE I need to lose myself in something else,
something dirty,
something that will certainly degrade my health.
That's why we're out,
getting loud and on a hype.
I've got my team by my side
And I won't let anything bring me down.
Not tonight.

I can see Ralph out the corner of my eye,
he's clearly loving life,
cutting shapes like he was making Christmas pies,
you know the little ones that you pack mince inside
that come in any kind of shape and size and
fuck it I'm chatting shit – man I must be high.

Well now seems an appropriate time
to introduce you to the team.
You've got Paul.

PAUL 'Iya.

JESSIE The lovable type,
never after a fight,
whereas Donna's a bit of a drama queen.

DONNA Fuck off!

JESSIE They're together you see,
since we were about sixteen,
but it's never felt like that to me.
You've met Ralph already,

RALPH Y'right?

JESSIE He works in tele,
    kind of boring by day
    but by night he comes alive
    and when he does he is deadly.

    I say that in a nice way,
    see these are my closest mates.
    Always top of their game
    and when someone's not
    we're all there because we all feel their pain.

    Call me insane
    but we share a bond
    that goes beyond
    any kind of physical means
    Joni said 'we are stardust'
    but I think we're made of more than that.
    I think we're made of stardust and dreams.

DONNA Oi Jessie, hurry up we're gonna miss the start!

JESSIE Fuck I almost forgot!
    I was too busy living in the sky,
    contemplating life,
    I'd lost the plot!
    See apart from getting fucked and forgetting life
    we've come to see Donna's mate on her opening night;
    the launch of her new EP
    on the biggest stage she's ever played live.

    Donna grabs my hand tight
    and guides me through
    a claustrophobic crowd of mostly men
    but every now and then
    a female comes into sight.
    We reach the front and head to the right,
    end up next to the speaker
    which is a little easier

with less people on both sides.
I feel free, energised
and ready to embrace the ride...
just as she steps into the light.

Spotlight on **ALLIE**.

She flashes a smile supernova bright,
that dazzles the crowd,
and has them soaking up her energy
like they were electrolytes.
Drop-dead gorgeous, she steps up to the mic,
the guitar plays and through the stage haze
I see a glint in her eye.
She looks left, then right,
then opens her mouth
and what comes out – christ.

> **ALLIE**
> HURRICANE HURRICANE
> PICTURES
> KNOCKING DOWN BESIDE ME
> SUGARCANE SUGARCANE
> SCRIPTURES
> BEING SCYTHED AND TAKEN IN
> WINDOWPANE WINDOWPANE
> DREAMING
> THE BREEZE OF MILD
> TEMPTATION
> AHHHHH OHHHH
> CRACK COCAINE CRACK COCAINE
> FEELINGS
> IT'S WHO YOU ARE IT'S SEEPING
> IN
>
> IT'S NOT ABOUT INCRIMINATION
> IT'S ALL ABOUT INSINUATION
> YOUR SILENCE MAKES MY
> STOMACH POUND

ALLIE *(cont.)*
YOUR VIOLENCE COMES FROM
THE UNDERGROUND
RECALLING YOU DON'T STOP ME
FEELING
IT OPENS UP THE HEART THAT'S
HEALING
IT'S A BIG LIFE NOW
IT'S A BIG LIFE NOW

JESSIE And we dance.

AND I'M COMING FOR YOU
Beat kicks in heavy, dark and low.

IT'S NOT ABOUT INCRIMINATION
IT'S ALL ABOUT INSINUATION
YOUR SILENCE MAKES MY
STOMACH POUND
YOUR VIOLENCE COMES FROM
THE UNDERGROUND
RECALLING YOU DON'T STOP ME
FEELING
IT OPENS UP THE HEART THAT'S
HEALING
IT'S A BIG LIFE NOW
IT'S A BIG LIFE NOW
AND I'M COMING FOR YOU

She's on for about an hour
but it's over way too soon.
The way she filled the room
I can't explain it –
it's like she gripped me with each tune.
Spoke to me like I was the only person there
and danced with me like she didn't care.

What was her name?

DONNA What?

JESSIE Her name – the singer? What was her name?

DONNA Allie Touch.

JESSIE Allie Touch.

How can you forget a name like that?

I wanna tell her she's great,
I wanna tell her she blew me away,
I wanna tell her that she's an artist
and I'm artist and somehow
we should collaborate.
Before Donna makes my day
and screams in my ear.

DONNA We're heading back to Allie's place.

JESSIE Then a short bus ride away
we find ourselves in the living room
of Allie's flat on Gipton estate.
Vodka in glass, coke up our nose
then someone picks up the guitar and plays.
And Allie,
for the second time tonight,
blows me away.

> **ALLIE**
> THINK OF THE TIME
> A SHORT TIME PASSED A LONG
> TIME LEAVING
> WHEN I THOUGHT THINGS WERE
> FINE
> NOW MY HEART'S GOT ME
> WONDERING
> WHAT EVEN IS THE MEANING OF
> THIS ASSEMBLING
> OR WHATEVER IT IS THAT GETS
> YOUR HEART TREMBLING

> ALLIE *(cont.)*
> A DAY IN THE LIFE OF A GIRL
> WITH NO NAME
> ADDICTED TO STRIFE LIKE A BUG
> YOU INFLAME

RALPH Smashed it Allie!

DONNA I love that one.

JESSIE Allie's great when she's up close
none of that bullshit thanks for coming guys.
It's her night tonight and she fuckin' knows.

PAUL What about this one!

> PAUL *plays.*

RALPH Come off it Paul, no one wants your dad music.

DONNA Leave him alone.

PAUL He's just jealous.

JESSIE That were proper different to what you did earlier.
I love it!

ALLIE Yeah it's cool.

RALPH You should do more acoustic stuff.

JESSIE You should.

ALLIE My producer wants me to keep it electronic.

RALPH Your producer's a twat. Thinks he knows about music
'cause he done a course.

ALLIE But he's got the contacts.

JESSIE Well use him, then move on.

ALLIE That's the plan. He wants me to move to London so I'm
gonna go down there to see how it goes.

JESSIE Dead pricey, though.

ALLIE It's alright actually, I found one of those warehouse shares. We're having a housewarming, you lot should come!

RALPH Not around mate.

DONNA We'll be there!

PAUL Yeah sounds like a right laugh.

ALLIE They're looking for acts I think, if anyone wants to play?

RALPH Jessie, get on that!

JESSIE Fuck off! I can paint if that helps?

ALLIE What, like paintings?

RALPH No...fences. Course paintings.

PAUL She's an artist.

DONNA Yeah, you've done artwork for gigs and stuff before!

JESSIE It's all the way in London though.

ALLIE Trust me, it'll be worth it. The last one was a proper rave.

JESSIE Dunno if I can really...

ALLIE Just stay at mine? We've got loads of space.

JESSIE The thought crosses my mind,
now's really not the time.

Donna catches my eye.
and silently asks if I'm alright,
which kind of pisses me off,
seeing as I'm having a good time.
I ignore her.

You gonna do the same set as tonight?

ALLIE More or less. Might switch it up a bit.

JESSIE I wish I were musical. My mum used to play a lot. She was incredible! She played in a Folk band for a bit.

ALLIE Does she still play?

JESSIE I'm not sure.

Beat.

ALLIE Are you into Folk?

JESSIE I love it. When I was little I was always singing, 'We are stardust'.

ALLIE Joni Mitchell – Woodstock.

JESSIE I always think about that, it's mad. We *are* stardust. Literally nothing but stardust and dreams.

RALPH That's so fucking lame.

JESSIE Fuck off!

DONNA Don't be nasty.

RALPH Oi, Paul, play something a bit more funky, I'm fallin' asleep with this shit.

PAUL *plays something different.*

Allie, jump on this one with me!

ALLIE Go on then.

RALPH Ralph and Allie
Also known as Rallie.

Coming off the top!
Here we go!

RALPH *starts to freestyle.*

Yeah
and we're in Allie's flat
Paul's on the gui-tar
Ralph with the rap

you know we're out all night
Allie hit us with the hook
that will set the room alight

ALLIE *jumps in with an improvised chorus.*

She follows by humming the melody.

> **ALLIE**
> BOY YOU GOT ME FEELING
> LIKE A GLASS HALF EMPTY
> PROBLEM WITH THE LOGIC
> I LOVE DRINKING PLENTY
> I LOVE DRINKING PLENTY
> I LOVE DRINKING PLENTY

DONNA Are you ok?

JESSIE Yeah, I'm fine!

DONNA You sure you're alright?

JESSIE I'm fine.

DONNA I just want you to know I love you.

RALPH Allie smashed it tonight,
burnt up the stage
like I might do a mic

Donna whispering and shit
bumming off with Jessie
while they have a little bitch.

DONNA Fuck off!

JESSIE Why're you such a dickhead, Ralph?

RALPH I'm only joking
now come and have a line,
Allie hit us with the chorus
one more time!

> **ALLIE**
> BOY YOU GOT ME FEELING
> LIKE A GLASS HALF EMPTY
> PROBLEM WITH THE LOGIC
> I LOVE DRINKING PLENTY

ALLIE *(cont.)*
I LOVE DRINKING PLENTY
I LOVE DRINKING PLENTY

BOY YOU GOT ME FEELING
LIKE A GLASS HALF EMPTY
PROBLEM WITH THE LOGIC
I LOVE DRINKING PLENTY
I LOVE DRINKING PLENTY
I LOVE DRINKING PLENTY

JESSIE I let their voices fade behind me
as I slip, unnoticed, out the door
and into the empty streets,
where I can breathe
with no one around.
I'm no fun when I'm like this,
stuck in a mood,
and I really don't want to bring
the rest of the room down.

Music takes over before fading out into an alarm clock.

I roll over to my alarm going off for work.
Lucky I booked it off
because my head fucking hurts
and I'm ready to throw up.
11AM on a Saturday morning
and I'm feeling rough.
I think back to last night,
it blurs out. Cracked lips. Dry mouth.
So I get myself a glass of water
to wash away the shame.
As I pass the empty room
I feel the sadness rise again.
I stop in the door frame.
See the bed made,

and the clothes poking out the wardrobe.
The bathrobe on the back of the door
and the battered brown loafers
Left out on the floor.

Everything's just how he left it
making it feel like an untouched shrine.
I feel disrespectful as I go through his things
even though now they're technically mine
I make a few piles in a line on the bed.
As I do I can't get that sound out of my head,
the song Allie started with,
it sings softly in the background of my mind
as I uncover things from the past
which he couldn't leave behind.

At the bottom of the wardrobe
there's a box labelled Jess
and yes, what's inside
isn't exactly hard to guess.
There's a small framed photo of me and him,
one that I've not seen before.
And tucked in between my teddy
and a couple of old school reports,
is a water painting of me, him and mum.
It's one I must of done when I were young,
because I've made my parents superheroes
and put me in my favourite clothing, Fifties style.
I must have recently watched *Grease*,
which makes my lips twitch to a smile.

Something I've not done sober for a while.

I head for the kitchen
to make a cup of something hot.
But not before I blue-tack
the painting to his window,

right in the middle, at the top.

I pop down the stairs
and pass the post
piling up on the doormat.
It's mostly just junk
and bills that seem to thicken.

But as I turn my back
the letterbox drops
another envelope.
Handwritten.

It's addressed to dad.
It's from mum.
I can't believe it.
We've not spoken in...

She says she wants to see me
whether dad wants her to or not
then she has a go at him
asking why the phone's been blocked
before she signs off
with her phone number...
Which is different to the one I've got.
But written in the top right
is something I'd tried to
find out for a long time.
A return address.

Flat 4, 32 Kilburn High Road, NW6 6PP

I can't believe...
All this time I thought she didn't give a toss
that she'd left us both in a split second
and not looked back.
But it was Dad's fault that the phone was blocked
that meant she wasn't able to get in contact.

I feel uprooted, void of something big,
an unearthed connection to my roots
and now I have this urge to dig.
I think about dad's room that's not longer his
and that painting on the window pane
that I did as a kid.
Then down at the handwriting
that I don't recognise.

And that need to dig gets deeper.

A text comes through.

RALPH Ey up squadron, meeting at 7 down't boozer for a couple
and then see where the night takes us! Hope you've not
forgot and you can handle two on the trot! Otherwise, it's
at least a million years till we'll get another chance! See ya
there! Big love. R.Kid (AKA Ralph)

JESSIE Fuck! I had forgot
and I'm really not feeling two nights on the trot.
But Ralph's fucking off to Norway for like forever.
Don't ask why Norway, I think he thinks it's clever.

RALPH Learn an unusual language.

JESSIE He said.

RALPH Because you never know when you might need it.

JESSIE I mean, that logic is flawed on so many levels
but you could never make him believe it.
Knowing him he'll be alright.
If it were me I'd be back overnight.
But Ralph will just soak up his new life.

I have to go.
I've known him since we were kids
looking down rabbit holes,
playing knock-a-door-run,
prank-calling people's home phones

and doing other things that were dumb.
Being right little shits.
And actually now I think of it,
him being around
I'm really gonna miss.

Soundscape of a not-so-great club.

I drink in the atmosphere
of the not-so-great place
Ralph has chosen to end
his final night in England in.
It's one of those classic dive bars,
with your drink in a plastic glass
and a strong smell of someone's arse
that seems to linger as they pass.

Donna is, as always, at least an hour late
and the rest of the crowd?
Well there's me, Paul
and a couple of Ralph's work mates.
You see everyone we know,
or used to know, has either fucked off,
is fucked up or has a baby so...
This is it, I guess.
But Ralph doesn't seem to mind.
Course not, he always has a good time.

Music takes over and they dance.

After the night gets six drinks and four shots good
we find ourselves outside,
trying to decide
between cocaine or food.
Coke wins of course on an occasion like this
and before we know it
we're back at Ralph's, still pissed
with a bag of tinnies and a packet of powder.

And we descend into reminiscing for hours.
From stupid tricks, to funny bits, to little ticks
we take a trip down memory lane,
and once again I can feel that pain rising.
I look at Donna and Paul. My rocks.
My mountains that will never fall.
My soldiers that will always stand tall
before Paul announces something
that surprises us all.

PAUL Donna and I are getting married.

DONNA We are. He popped the question last week. Took him long enough.

PAUL Well I wanted to do it properly.

JESSIE That's great.
I say,
and I can hear how unconvincing I sound.
But everyone's so coked up
no one notices anything other
than what they're on about.

PAUL I took her to school, you know, 'cause that's where we met and I got Mr. Simmons to let us use the maths classroom where I used to sit behind her and poke her with my pencil and kick the back of her chair.

DONNA It were really thoughtful.

JESSIE Sounds it.

Why aren't I happy?
I should feel over the moon,
I should be bouncing round the room,
I should be overjoyed that in a few months
they will be bride and groom.

PAUL I'd got all of the different things I used to throw at her from WH Smiths. Rubbers, pencils, a compass, rulers, chewed

up bits of paper and I blue-tacked them to the interactive
whiteboard so that they spelt 'Will You Marry Me?' And
then I had a bucket of spare ones so she had to blue-tack
her answer on underneath so it were like an interactive
experience.

JESSIE That's so lovely. Congratulations guys.

Paul's proposal sounds shit.
Like so shit, it makes me sick
that Donna even said yes to it.
But that's not the bit that I care about.
I can't shake this feeling that
everything's slipping away
and now all I can do is grasp
hopelessly at thin air.

I actually don't care! You know.

The joy in the room turns to tense focus.
The shock hangs for a moment.
Paul looks like he's been hit
by a million ton lorry
before Donna says:

DONNA Sorry?

JESSIE I don't care. I say again.

And I take a look at my friends.
A long hard look,
from top to bottom.
And I think out loud.

We don't have anything in common.
And this habit is rotten
and no I haven't forgotten
that we grew up together but that's it?
Isn't it?

I mean apart from that there's nowt?

DONNA Jess what're you on about? You're talking shit!

JESSIE I'm being pensive.

PAUL You're being really offensive.

JESSIE Well I'm sorry Paul but I meant it!
And that song begins to play again
in the background of my mind.
Allie Touch.

I'm talking about us!
I mean this.
It's a pile of shit,
our relationship.
You two are getting married,

Ralph you're just fucking off
and no one gave a toss
how I was feeling when
my Dad topped himself.
Did you?

DONNA That's not true?

JESSIE Isn't it though?
It were three weeks ago
and yet it feels like for you
it were a lifetime away
and I'm not trying to say
that you guys should
put your lives on hold
but don't rub it in my face.
Fuck! I'm sick of this place.
Where you either fuck off or shack up
with the first bloke you've found,
regardless of how shit his proposal is,
and no one around
has any ambition to get off of the ground.

And I'm sick of it.

This repetitive negative fuckery just for the hell of it
aimlessly wandering blind to the world out there just 'cause
you're scared of it
I'm hopelessly dreaming for something with meaning and
you don't want shares in it.
Sitting wasting my life like I don't really care for it
I'm feeling done with this place I grew up look I think I
need air from it.
You irrelevant people are holding me back.

This small world,
these small minds,
with small dreams
that are not mine.

I need more than what you want.
I need more than this.

And I look at the room we're in
and the people that I suddenly
don't recognise anymore.
The carpet on the floor
that I've trod a thousand times before
feels alien.
I can feel I'm going pale again.

DONNA Jessie, sit down. You look sick.

JESSIE I know Donna's speaking
but I can barely hear shit.
I turn and walk out the door, quick.
No one shouts after me
and I think, fuck. That's it.

The night's fresh air
hits me like a cold flannel on hot skin.
I zip my Adidas jacket up to my chin

and phone in hand I try to decide
whether I should give mum a ring.

I can't call her like this
freaking out, and completely off my tits.
It's not right.

I text her instead,
saying I miss her a lot
and perhaps in the morning
she could give me a ring
and in the glow of a lone street light
I'm reminded of a song
that her band used to sing

> **JESSIE**
> THE CITY LIGHTS
> ARE OH SO BRIGHT
> AND I CAN FEEL YOU WITH ME
> I CAN FEEL YOU WITH ME
> TONIGHT.
>
> THE CITY LIGHTS
> ARE HERE TONIGHT
> AND I CAN SEE YOU WITH ME
> I CAN SEE YOU WITH ME
> TONIGHT.

I look at my phone. It's half three.
Fuck me. I'm lucky.
Normally it's later when I leave Ralph's.
Normally it's light and I can hear the birds sing
but not now.
Now all I can hear is the dead of night.
As I wander the streets of Leeds
the darkness sings back to me
not long now 'till it's light.

JESSIE AND MUM
THE CITY LIGHTS
ARE OH SO BRIGHT
AND I CAN FEEL YOU WITH ME
I CAN FEEL YOU WITH ME
TONIGHT.

THE CITY LIGHTS
ARE HERE TONIGHT
AND I CAN SEE YOU WITH ME
I CAN SEE YOU WITH ME
TONIGHT.

WHAT IS WRONG HERE
WHAT IS WRONG WITH ME
I AM LOSING MY SANITY
AND I'M FILLED WITH SUCH
DOUBT AND I
CANNOT GET OUT
THEN I SEE THE CITY LIGHTS
THEY MAKE ME SMILE AND I
SIT OUTSIDE AND I
LISTEN FOR A WHILE
'CAUSE I'M NEVER ALONE
WHEN THE PEOPLE ARE PLAYING
I'M HAPPY AS LONG
AS THEY'RE SINGING THEIR
TUNE
I'VE MADE UP MY MIND
THAT THERE'S NO SENSE IN
STAYING
SO TONIGHT I'LL JUST WONDER
AND STARE AT THE MOON

My phone beeps, must be Donna
calling to say sorry for being a cunt
but when I take out my phone
lit on the screen is the word mum.

MUM Hi love, it's so good to hear from you. I'm glad you got
my letter! I know your dad's angry for what I did but he
shouldn't have blocked the phone. How are you both? Is
your dad ok? It would be lovely to see you sometime soon.
Love mum.

JESSIE It hits me like a ton of bricks!
How could I not think of this
and just let it slip
from out my head.
I've been so wound up in me
that I didn't see that of course
she doesn't know that dad is dead.

I can't tell her by text.
That's fucked. I have to see her.
I need to go.
Then the next thing I know,
I hear the sound of the dial tone
Before –

ALLIE Hello?

JESSIE Allie! I want to come with you to London!

ALLIE Ok...

JESSIE Is that alright?

ALLIE Course. How come you changed your mind?

JESSIE I found this address.
On this letter.

From Mum.
It's in London.
And since meeting you
since my dad did what he had to do
I've been feeling like there's something missing
something extra.

And then I got this text and –

ALLIE Jessie, you fucked again?

JESSIE Yeah.

ALLIE Look, it's late.
       Just get home safe.
       Ok?

JESSIE But I'm alright to come with ya, yeah?

ALLIE Course.
       I'm getting the train in the morning.

JESSIE I thought you were going in a couple of days?

ALLIE My plans changed.
       Meet me down there if you want?

       Jess?

JESSIE Yes! I will.
       That's great.
       See you soon, yeah?

ALLIE See you soon mate.

JESSIE I make my way home.
       There's tension in my bones
       as the key turns in the lock.
       I daren't stop.
       Just grab mum's letter off the side,
       sunglasses to cover my eyes
       from the early morning light
       as I wait for the taxi I just ordered.
       Then thirty minutes later
       I'm standing, a little awkward
       in the queue at the station.
       Destination?

       London.

       I get to the ticket window
       buy my ticket and go

and before I know it I'm sat rigid
on the red seats of my overpriced train.

I google Soundcloud, Allie Touch
squinting at my phone
in the bright light of day
I select a song,
put my headphones in
and press play.

And the music takes me away.

         ALLIE
         INDIGO SUNRISE
         SHOULD MEAN A NEW DAY
         A THIN LIGHT THAT'S SHINING
         AN OVER FULL ASH TRAY
         HARD SKULL
         THAT'S SOFTLY SOAKED IN
         SPIRITS
         MAKES A PAINTING ON MY
         CEILING
         AS I SWIFTLY DRIFT AWAY

         AND I SLEEP THEN
         AND I'M DREAMING
         AND I'M RUNNING LIKE A
         DICKHEAD
         THROUGH THE SPARKLY CITY OF
         LONDON
         AND I SEE HER
         AND I'M BREATHING
         SHE IS LAUGHING LIKE SHE
         USED TO
         AND I TOTALLY BELIEVE SHE'S
         NEVER LEAVING

I open my eyes and see fields of grass
and rapeseed in great yellow patches

amongst the green
and every now and then
a building, or a town,
or a factory can be seen.
The stations run by in a blur.
My eyes hurt from lack of sleep
and my back's riddled with stress.
I take out the letter from mum
and I see the address is slightly stained
and gradually the train
feels like it's getting smaller,
like it's going to break.
I find a pen in my bag
and jot down mum's address
on the back of my hand quickly,
Flat 4, 32 Kilburn High Road, NW6 6PP.
Then I hear myself shout I want to get off!
When they say over the tannoy:

TRAIN GUARD   The next station-stop
will be London Kings Cross.

Please make sure you have all your belongings with you
when you leave the train. Thank you for travelling with
us today and I wish you a pleasant onward journey. Once
again the next station-stop will be London Kings Cross.

JESSIE   I burst out onto the platform
like water from an over-pressured tap.
I look around and think thank fuck for that.
I've no idea where I'm going though
and the streams of suits are too hectic
so I bosh the rest of that coke
and through the feeling of focus
I see a sign – exit.

I grab my bag, roll a fag out of my backy,
smoke it when I get outside

as I try and flag down a taxi.
I end up getting one of those black cabs
with a geezer of a driver.
I show him Allie's address and he says:

TAXI DRIVER I'll do it twice as quick love if ya tip me a fiver.

JESSIE My brain doesn't register it's a joke,
so I nod in sincerity and we go.
And the streets of London flash by,
before we end up on an industrial estate
that looks like the kind of place
you wouldn't want to walk through at night.

Is this it?

TAXI DRIVER This is the address you gave me.
Not sure which one Unit 2 is though.
Probably one of those.

JESSIE He points to what looks like a factory for clothes
or meat or something...but not a home.
I thank him, pay him and go,
walk down the road
and up to a large metal door
big enough to fit a van through.
And right next to it
printed in white paint against blue
is the confirmation in block capitals:

UNIT 2.

I tentatively knock on the big iron door,
then hit it again with a bit more force
before someone pokes their head
out of a window on the top floor.

JIM Round the side.

JESSIE He shouts and then he's gone.
So I wander round the building

where there's a smaller wooden door
with a buzzer on that I go to ring,
just as the door flings open revealing him.
The guy from the window.

I'm Jess. We haven't met. I'm a friend of Allie's?

JIM Who's Allie?

JESSIE She's moving in here? Today I think?

JIM Oh you mean the singer girl? Didn't think she was in 'till
tomorrow?

JESSIE Her plans changed. She's coming this afternoon I think.

JIM Oh right. First I've heard of it. You her mate?

JESSIE Yeah. Sort of. She said I could crash for a bit.

It were quite last minute.

He looks at me for a second
and I can tell he's wondering if I'm lying or not.

JIM Well you better come in then.

JESSIE He says finally. Realising that the connections
are far too far-fetched to be a lie.
He steps back, arm stretched out
to keep the door propped open as I step inside.
At first it's dark with little light,
I'm in a corridor which he points me down and says –

JIM Turn right.

JESSIE And when I do, wow what a sight.

It's a big open-plan warehouse
with steps directly on my left
but straight ahead is like,
what I can only describe
as the shape of a grand entrance hall...
except the warehouse version.

Doors line both walls on either side.
I count eight. Four on the left four on the right
and at the end it opens out to a kitchen
with three fridges
and the whole place is lit with strip lights.

Up those stairs,
when I came in on the left hand side,
is a balcony that sits on top of the rooms
and goes right round the building
so you've got a three sixty view
down into the entrance hall.
They've got pool, darts and table football
and a big set of decks with records lining the wall.

JIM I'm Jim. By the way.

JESSIE Jess. Do you DJ?

JIM I mess about.

JESSIE What do you play?

JIM All sorts. But mostly House.

JESSIE Are these records yours?

JIM Course. I'll get them out.

JESSIE And he begins to play.

House music plays. It's soft. Low.

I feel a sense of pleasure tingle down my spine
as I watch his hands glide across the decks.
It kind of makes me horny but not for sex,
like I'm not wet, I'm just impressed.
Less stressed, I start to dance and so does he,
slowly.
Which one's Allie's room?

JIM That one on the end, next to the kitchen.

JESSIE Can I have a look?

JIM Yeah. Course.

JESSIE I wander up to the cabin-like room
that has no character at all.
Still though, it's nice enough
even if it is a little small.

JIM So what do you do for work?

JESSIE Nothing. At the moment. I'm an artist. I mean I haven't
trained or done uni or anything I just... Like it.

JIM Is that why you're in London?

JESSIE No, I'm here to – um – I guess, to find someone.

JIM Fair enough. Do you know where to look?

Looking at the back of her hand.

JESSIE Flat 4, 32 Kilburn High Road, NW6 6PP

JIM That's precise.

I'm actually heading to Wembley tomorrow so I could
probably give you a lift if you like?

JESSIE I can see he's rolling a spliff
in his room which is across
the entrance hall from me.
And the thought of smoking it
makes me start to crash again, quickly.
I lie down on the bed even though it's not made.

Er...yeah that would be great.
How come you're heading that way?

JIM I'm picking up a rig to kit this place out for tomorrow night.

JESSIE I think he sees the confusion on my face at the word
rig, so he clarifies.

JIM Speakers. Big ones.

JESSIE What's happening tomorrow night?

JIM We're having a party. A housewarming to welcome the new people in!

JESSIE Course. I forgot about that. Who else is new?

I can feel my eyes closing as I start to doze off.

JIM Well there's the singer girl.

JESSIE Allie, she's top.

JIM Then there's a guy called Paul and a lady called Donna. And there's also Ralph.

Then there's me, Tom and Helen.

JESSIE Tom and Helen. That's my mum and dad's name.

I mumble, not quite sure if the words have made it past my lips.

And I think of home.
Think of my friends,
think of what I said,
how I left things with them

and I feel sick.

I bolt upright and shut the door quick,
after a short glance at Jim
who's occupied with his spliff.

I find Donna in contacts
as I take out my phone

DONNA Hello?

JESSIE Donna. It's Jess.

DONNA I know.

JESSIE Look I wanted to ring to apologise for what I said.

I'm sorry.

DONNA You done?

JESSIE I guess.

DONNA Great, bye then.

JESSIE Donna wait. Don't be like that –

DONNA Who do you think you are? Talking to us like that?

JESSIE I know, I'm sorry. I really am. But...

DONNA But what?

JESSIE You lot... You don't care about –

DONNA Course we do. You just don't want to move on.

JESSIE That's not true.

DONNA Life goes on.

JESSIE My dad killed himself, Donna.

DONNA Because of you!
  Until you accept that
  there's nothing we can do.
  You have to move on.
  And going to London
  in search of your mum
  isn't going to fix anything.

JESSIE How do you know I'm in London?

DONNA Look Jessie,
  your mum doesn't want to see you,
  and she doesn't want you turning up
  at her house.

JESSIE You don't know that.

DONNA I do.

JESSIE Oh piss off! You always think you know what's best but you don't. You don't know nothing.

DONNA There you go again, lashing out at me when I'm trying to help.

JESSIE I'm not, you're just...

DONNA I just want what's best for you, Jessie.

JESSIE Why are you being so out of order then?

DONNA Because you're a selfish little girl lost in a world that's
  far too big for you –

JESSIE I'm not –

DONNA And I can't have someone in my life who's as negative
  as you are.

JESSIE Donna –

DONNA Don't call me again.

JESSIE I fold onto the bed,
  my body crumpling into the mattress
  as the line goes dead
  and any sense of strength drains from me.
  Painfully I let the loneliness overtake
  as I drift away,
  tears provide little warmth
  as they run down my face
  and the only solace I find
  is my mind shutting up for the day.

  I wake up, drenched in sweat,
  to the sound of knocking on wood.

  Who is it?

JIM It's Jim.

JESSIE Jim, of course.
  My becomes clearer
  with that thought.
  I open the door.

JIM Are you alright?

JESSIE I must look a fucking mess,
  drenched in sweat
  and probably stinking too...

But I style it out by saying

Yeah, fine thanks. You?

Fucking smooth.

JIM   Yeah. Um, d'you want that lift?
      I'm probably gonna head out in ten.

JESSIE   What time is it?

JIM   About 3 p.m.

JESSIE   Fucking hell!

I skip the shower
even though I smell like a rodent,
opt for a breakfast of fags
wash with deodorant,
and ten minutes later
I'm sat in the front of Jim's van
staring at the little man
hanging from his rear view mirror.
When I hear Donna's voice
clear as day, say –

DONNA   Your mum doesn't want to see you,
        and she doesn't want you
        turning up at her house.

JESSIE   What if she's right?
         If I turn up all smiles
         with the hope that she's
         excited to see me.
         And she tells me to fuck off.

Then I think of the letter she sent
and the thought settles my mind.

Jim's van a transit.
White.
The classic geezer-mobile.

Not that Jim's like that.
I ask him why he's got it and he says –

JIM I do odd jobs for cash.
Man with a van type thing.
Plus it's good for moving stuff about.

JESSIE Thanks for helping me out.

JIM No problem. Do you want picking up later?

JESSIE He says as we pull up on Kilburn High Road.
That would be top. But only if you've got time?

JIM Yeah, that's fine. Should be about an hour.

JESSIE I step down out of the van
that's pulled up in a bus stop behind the 328.
I turn to say thank you before he surprises me and says –

JIM Good luck mate. I hope it goes ok.

JESSIE Thanks.
I say.
It weren't so much what he said
but the way he said it
that left me slightly dazed
as he pulled away.

I try to find my bearings
as I locate the right place.
In my mind it looks like a big town house
that has been divided into many flats
but when I arrive at number 32,
well, it couldn't be further from that.

My fantasy house
with five floors rising up
quickly fades away
as I'm confronted by a Starbucks.

Resting on top
of the corporate coffee shop
is a high-rise of modern-ish
looking flats painted blue
with those shit kind of balconies
that don't have any room
and plants hanging off them
to try and improve
the relatively dismal view.

I wonder if she's in there?
And if she is I wonder if she cares?
And if she does I wonder if she's prepared
to hear what I've got to say.

My finger shakes over the buzzer to flat 4
but I can't block out what Donna said before.

DONNA Your mum doesn't want to see you,
and she doesn't want you turning up
at her house.

JESSIE Yes she does.

My finger presses down.
I hear the buzzer sound
and immediately a woman's voice
comes out of the speaker.

MUM Hello?

JESSIE And I'm struck dumb.

Mum?

MUM Jessie?

JESSIE She replies with uncertainty...

Yeah. Mum, it's me.

MUM Jessie. What are you doing here?

JESSIE I wanted to – ask you...to tell you –

And I don't know where to start, how to begin...
Mum can you let me in?

MUM I'm not sure if I can, Jess.

JESSIE What? Why?

MUM Look you shouldn't be here. It's not safe for you.

JESSIE What do you mean?

MUM It's why I moved. To keep you safe.

JESSIE From what?

MUM Jessie, please just leave! I mean it.

JESSIE And her voice is getting agitated.
She's almost in a whisper now.

MUM I'm sorry, I'm sure you want some answers
and I'm happy to talk but just not now... Please!

JESSIE And then I hear another voice
come out the speaker.

MAN Who's that?

MUM Jessie, run!
It's no one –

JESSIE Mum?

MAN Who are you talking to?

JESSIE Mum?

But she's gone.
I press the buzzer again straight away
but no one answers.
I press it again without delay
until I hear over the relay:

MAN Hello?

JESSIE I can hear mum in the background too.

MUM Jessie please leave, you don't know what he'll do.

JESSIE Put mum on!

MAN What?

MUM Jessie go!

JESSIE No! I'm her daughter. What's going on?
And I hear mum scream.
What have you done?

MAN Nothing. What's wrong? Are you lost?

JESSIE He says and his tone mocks...
I can tell he's nasty piece of work.

If you've hurt her I'll fucking kill you!
I feel my anger surge,
so I buzz again heart racing

MAN If you ring my buzzer one more time
I'm gonna come down there
and smash your face in.

JESSIE Where's my mum?

MAN I don't care! Now fuck off.

MUM Leave her alone!

MAN You're taking the piss now!

JESSIE Mum! Are you ok.

MAN Go away!

MUM Jessie!

JESSIE Mum!

MAN Shut up!

MUM Leave her alone!

JESSIE I hear a thump
over the speaker phone.

A dull hit, followed quick
by a choked-up scream
that mum tries to swallow.

MUM I'm sorry!

JESSIE I stare at my reflection
in the glass door, my tight jaw
locked on my dazed face
as I take a slight step away.

I turn around and see a crowd
of strangers staring my way.

I've just been witness to domestic abuse.

His eyes open wide.

STRANGER Is it an emergency?

JESSIE Yes!

STRANGER Then call 999.

JESSIE Fine!

POLICE OFFICER Police, Fire Brigade or Ambulance?

JESSIE Police.

POLICE OFFICER What's the emergency?

JESSIE My mum, she's been abused in her home!

POLICE OFFICER What's the address please?

JESSIE I look at the back of my hand but it's rubbed off.
I know the postcode ends in a P.

POLICE OFFICE In a P?

JESSIE And it starts with an NW – It's Kilburn High Road.

POLICE OFFICER Do you think she's in immediate danger?

JESSIE Yes I heard it! Heard her over the tannoy.

POLICE OFFICER Tannoy?

JESSIE To her flat. I buzzed her flat – I haven't seen her in ages
and she – I heard a thud –

POLICE OFFICER You heard a thud?

JESSIE It was like someone being hit.

POLICE OFFICER Do you know which flat it is?

JESSIE It's near Victoria Road – flat four.
If I wait for you by her door
will you send someone?

POLICE OFFICER They're already on their way.

JESSIE They stop at the signal of my frantic arm
I direct them to the door
where the officer presses the buzzer with his palm.
There's no answer.
He must have heard the sirens
and seen me waiting at the door!
Fuck! I should have thought about that
and hidden more.

I tell them about mum.
They said there's nothing that can be done now
but they have my details written down
and they'll check back tomorrow
in case they've just gone out.

As I watch them leave
feeling reluctant to let them go,
I've got a funny feeling that I know
he's still got mum inside his home.
I jog a little down the road
to see if I can see her through the window
but when I hear a scream –

MUM Get off me!

JESSIE I know exactly what it means

and I dart round the back to where the bins go.
There's a door that's been left slightly ajar
but a little further from that
I see mum's face in the back seat of a car.

MUM Jessie!

JESSIE She screams out of the back window!

MUM Be careful, he'll hurt you!

JESSIE Mum! I start to run!
Pushed on by the fear of what he might do
or what he might've already done!

The car speeds off
mocking me with it's back lights
when I notice on my right
is a rack of bikes
with one unlocked.
I barely stop,
just pull the bike out
and plant myself firmly on the seat
by now they're halfway down the street
so I press down hard with my feet
driven by the speed of my heart beat.

I fly up to the back of the car, my pace rapid
screaming at the back window in sheer panic

when I hear mum shout –

MUM Jessie, please! Help me!

JESSIE They easily overtake the car in front
and speed off faster than I can pedal.
I jump off the bike and slam it down
grounded by the sound
of concrete cracking against metal.

MUM Help me!

JESSIE She said
    her words ring in my head
    I pull out my phone
    but the fucking battery's dead.

    And then I think of Jim
    my heart rate slows at the thought of him.
    He'll know what to do.

    I head back to the High Road,
    flag a taxi at the top
    and a little while later I'm speed-walking across
    the industrial estate to Jim's place
    when I hear the sound of low bass
    rumble across the empty space.
    Fuck! The housewarming!

    I think of mum, kidnapped by that cunt
    and I can't stand the thought
    as I walk up to the big metal doors.
    Lit by the multicoloured lights
    that bleed through the windows on each floor.

    I push through the people spilling out of the door
    and burst right into the warehouse
    which is dressed like something
    I've never seen before!
    It's a full-on rave, with neon paint
    and fabric hanging from the ceiling
    reflecting light from an actual stage!

    It's been set up in what was the kitchen
    and the speaker system's
    so big the stage is bending in its resistance.
    I spot the DJ step up to his decks
    set up next to the speaker tower
    just as an MC picks up the mic
    and brings the packed warehouse

up to full power.

MC Alright, alright, alright,
from the front to the back
to the left to the right
everybody inside
let me see a signal,
let me see a sign!

We got a mad line-up for you lot tonight!
First up, in true UNIT 2 style
you ain't seen him for a while
but you know he's still your boy.
It's our very own resident DJ
DJ Roy!
'cause you know how we do.
This is UNIT 2.
Roy I'll leave the rest to you.
All my real ravers out there.

Are. You. Ready?

Alright then... Roy

RUN THAT

RIDDA RIDDA RIDDA RIDDA RUN IT DOWN
MILITANT RIDDEM REAL DUNGEON SOUND
RID IT ON THE RIDDEM THEN I RID IT ALL AROUND
I'M CHILLIN' FOR A LIVIN' I AIN'T GIVING THEM A POUND.
'CAUSE I AIN'T REALLY GOT A WAY WITH THE WORDS

JESSIE I barge my way through
the bouncing bodies and into Allie's room
which has become a den of fucked friends
racking up on her table top.
I open my mouth
to release a desperate shout
when one of the girls turns round
which forces a smile out.

ALLIE Jessie!

JESSIE Allie! Thank god I found you!

ALLIE Thank you so much for coming! You've arrived just in time!

JESSIE Allie! My mum –

ALLIE I'm about to play again, live!

JESSIE What?

ALLIE Me and Jim! He asked me when I got here today!

JESSIE I thought you came yesterday?

ALLIE Nah mate, today! You gonna come up with me on stage?!

JESSIE Wait! Allie, I really need to talk to you! Please –

ALLIE Come on! Up next it's me!

JESSIE And the MC on cue announces to the room:

MC Ladies and gentlemen
also opening the show tonight.
Straight after droppin' her first EP
a rising star fresh on the scene –

JESSIE Allie, my mum's in serious danger –

MC All the way from Leeds
the girl you're lucky to see
are you lot ready?!
Ladies and gentlemen give it up
for Allie Touch!

JESSIE And the place erupts!
Allie!

ALLIE
FEEL LIKE MY LEGS CANNOT
CARRY THIS WEIGHT
AND I CAN'T STOP RUNNING
THERE'S A DEMON COMING
AHH AHH

FEEL LIKE MY LUNGS ARE
CONSUMED BY DECAY
BUT I CAN'T STOP FIGHTING
AND IT'S SO INVITING
AHH AHHH

MC
RIDDA RIDDA RIDDA RIDDA RUN
IT DOWN
MILITANT RIDDEM REAL
DUNGEON SOUND
RID IT ON THE RIDDEM THEN I
RID IT ALL AROUND
I'M CHILLIN' FOR A LIVIN' I AIN'T
GIVING THEM A POUND.
'CAUSE I AIN'T REALLY GOT A
WAY WITH THE WORDS
BUT I'VE GOT A LOT TO SAY
WHEN I SPRAY IT ON THE VERSE
AND I DO IT ALL DAY EVERY DAY
TO BE HEARD
SOME CALL ME STRANGE –
ABSURD.
IT'S JUST ME FROM THE CRADLE
TO THE EARTH
'TILL I'M SIX FEET DEEP AND MY
FLAME'S BEEN BURNT
BUT WHY AM I THE ONE THEY
PUT THE BLAME ON FIRST?
GOT LOVE FOR THE GAME YOU
CAN TAKE MY WORD.
STILL TAKE THAT BUS FOR AN
EIGHTH OF HERB
CHEEKS STILL BLUSH WHEN I
MEET THAT BIRD
FEET STILL RUNNIN' SAME BEAT
UP CURB
THE STREETS OF LONDON I BEEN
SINCE BIRTH.

ALLIE
YOU TOLD ME
YOU TOLD ME, YOU PROMISED
ME
WAITED FOR YOU LIKE A
CREATURE OF NIGHT
I FOUND YOU
OOOOO YOU FRIGHTENED ME
INCH FROM YOUR TOUCH
YOU WERE SNATCHED OUT OF
SIGHT

JESSIE I can't focus or think straight
the crowd's so tight I can't
break through their tension
I know mum's in trouble
but there's nowt I can do
to get Jim's attention

And through all the noise
I hear mum's broken voice –

MUM Jessie help me!

JESSIE I'm trying mum!

I do my best to run.
As I push my way through the crowd,
Allie's crystal voice pouring out
like fire-water so loud it's causing
an ice-burning in my head,
and a wet-drought in my mouth,
I try and shout out
but the words are drowned down.

I come into Jim's sight
and his face fills with light
before it quickly turns
to bleak concern –

he can see the worry in my eyes.
It's almost a surprise when he runs forward
and pulls me up onto the stage
out of the packed crowd.

We need to go now.

JIM What's wrong?

JESSIE My mum, she's been kidnapped.

JIM Right, ok.

JESSIE I can see that he doesn't want to leave.
Instead he tries to lead me
to the back of the stage.

No! I've got to go!

JIM Maybe you should slow down a bit and wait.

JESSIE On the stage it's so loud
with Allie working the crowd
I try and pull away from Jim
but he's holding on tighter now.

JIM Come and look at this.

JESSIE No I've got to go it's important

JIM Just wait –

JESSIE When out of nowhere,
I see Donna's face.
She's standing next to Jim's decks,
in a green dress,
looking at me with an expression
that's less than impressed.

I don't have time for this.

I scream at her!

Go away and leave me alone

After what she said to me on the phone
I know I've no hope of her helping me out.

DONNA Jessie, what are you on about? Are you ok?

JESSIE I yank my arm hard away from Jim
freeing myself from him
and my head is overloading
with all the songs that Allie sings.

And mum's screaming –

MUM Jessie I'm running out of time!

JESSIE I don't know what to do,
I turn around to the rest of the room
and no one has a fucking clue!
They're all just dancing and laughing
and fucked up, I want them to shut up and get lost.
Pissed off I stumble over to the speakers
grab hold of the lever that's binding the strap
round the main body of the tower.
I hear Jim shout something but it's too late
as I see the speakers spray across the stage,
light as droplets from a shower.
They boulder around the place,
smashing into the floor,
the top ones break on contact
from falling with such force.
And everyone in the room
turns around to look at me.

And I stare back into the
vast ocean of their collective face.

Allie's dumb-struck
so I grab the mic that's fallen by her waist.

And into it,
connected to the last working speaker,

I say with a broken voice
that's weak and getting weaker:

My mum's in serious trouble. She's been kidnapped and I
think she's going to get hurt and I need someone to help
me. Please help me. It's not funny and I'm scared for her
and none of you believe me! HELP ME PLEASE.

I feel soft arms wrap around me
as I fall back into Jim,
I try to fight him but he wins.
I let him take me off the stage
and into a back room
and soon Donna comes in too.

DONNA Jessie, relax. I'm here for you. I'm going to take you
home.

JESSIE I need to find mum.

DONNA Jessie –

JESSIE She's been kidnapped by this man, she needs me to call
her or she's gonna get hurt, we have to get her! NOW! Why
won't anyone help me?

DONNA I know you must be scared. But you have to listen to me–

JESSIE There's no time! I just spoke to her

DONNA When?

JESSIE What?

DONNA When did you speak to her?

JESSIE Just now! I was on the phone to her!

DONNA Your phone's dead Jessie. I've been ringing it for ages.

JESSIE No it's –

DONNA Your mum's not here. She's not in London. Jessie, she
passed away last year.

JESSIE What? No – she's... Why are you saying that, Donna?

DONNA It's true, but it's ok because what we're gonna do –

JESSIE Fuck you.

DONNA I'm gonna take you home. You're gonna come stay with Paul and I. We've got a spare room.

JESSIE But – I – need mum.

DONNA I know you do. I can't imagine what you've been through. It must be so hard for you. But you have to trust me.

JESSIE I heard her voice!

DONNA I know –

JESSIE Why don't you believe me?

DONNA I do. I believe you heard her.

JESSIE So you're saying I'm mental? Crazy? That I don't know what's real?

DONNA Your mind's playing tricks on you, Jessie, that's all. You've been through a lot. And we've been shit friends. But we'll all be there for you now. I promise! Please, just come back with me and Paul.

JESSIE And Jim and Paul appear with my bags packed up.

The letter! She sent me a letter, yesterday!

What have you done with them, Donna?

DONNA Nothing, I promise Jessie.

JESSIE It's in my bag! Paul! In the front!

PAUL Jessie, it's not there.

JESSIE No... Donna, you're just fucking with me like you did on the phone.

DONNA We haven't spoke on the phone.

JESSIE We did. Last night. You said mum doesn't want to see me. You said it were my fault that dad died.

DONNA No I didn't and it's not! He wasn't able to cope with
what happened to your mum. He loved you. He did. So
much. But sometimes life gets the better of us.

Please, come home. Paul's not been drinking. He's gonna
drive us back.

JESSIE I look from Paul, to Donna, to Jim.
And confused and tired they give me no choice
but to give in.

We drive back home, slow.
Mum keeps telling me that I shouldn't go
but Donna's got my hand tight
as we drive through the black of night,
my cheeks, tear-stained, shine
from time to time with the reflection
of the street lights.
The radio plays the whole way home,
helping to block out mum's desperate tones
and providing an ambiance in the car
as we glide across the road.

Paul and Donna take me to their house
and put me in their spare room.
Over the next month or two
things get much worse.
My head hurts with voices
that don't make any sense
and the pent up emotion drives them day to day.
Sometimes they're nice. Sometimes they're funny.
But mostly they're evil with what they say.
They're nasty. They tell me that I'm shit.
Tell me they'll do horrible things
and that it's my fault that dad did what he did.

But although times seemed tough,
and I made it fucking hard,

Donna and Paul never gave up.
They helped me speak to the right people,
eat the right food,
they stuck by me when the voices were being crude
even stayed in the room
when I was screaming at them.

Working through it was confusing as fuck.
I went on psych meds
and I had to ask what the truth was
and what I'd made up
where I'd been, who I loved
and what was real about the world.

But what was real didn't made sense
with what the voices would think up
and although I'd known
the people around me growing up
There was still a lack of trust.

I thought they were conspiring against me
or involved in some kind of plot
I lost confidence in myself
and was frustrated
not being able to tell the mist from the fog.

It took many set backs
and arguments with myself
constant visits to doctors
and friends looking after my health.
Friends that make up my entire world.

But gradually, as the months went on
my thoughts, like trapped sand,
compressed into pearls
and I began to see clearly again.

Slowly I began to regain my life

and to Donna and Paul's surprise
I went back to the house
sat on his bed and I didn't cry.

You see, for the first time since he died
I was able to focus on why.
He felt so lost and alone
and no that wasn't my fault
or something that I should have known.
It were just impossible for him to cope.

And it made me think
that there are millions of people
on this island that will one day sink
on this planet that will one day be
engulfed by the sun
and one by one we will all
come to an end.

We are a blip. A spec of dust.
To be wiped off the face of time
like you might a bike chain's rust.
But to each of us, we are everything.

You see Joni almost had it right.
We *are* stardust.
But we are also so much more than that.
We are made of stardust and dreams.
All there actually is, is you and me
and we make our own choices in this reality.
See I can't help but think
that in the insignificance of it all
I feel more important than
I've ever felt before.
I am who I am
and you are who you are
so you do you, and I'll do me

and we'll go fucking far.

I think all my dad needed
was a sense of self, a sense of place.
You see when my mum passed
the world came crashing in
and straight away he crumbled.
But if someone had smiled
and told him it were ok
or just said I'm here to chat
if you think you need to mate.
Or said come round for a cup of tea
I'll put it in my favourite mug
or how about that shit karaoke
they do down at that dodgy pub.

Or even just said mate,
you look great.

Because you never know
who's in what sort of place.
And you might just end up being
that person's saving grace.

I look up at the superhero painting
on the window pane.
I pluck it down gently,
watching the blue-tack peel away.

I check the back and see the date
1998
I look at the front
see me, dad and mum
and out loud I say
I will never throw this away.

JIM What is it mate?

JESSIE And I think that if I wasn't doing

this emotional speech to all you pricks
I'd probably be over the moon
to hear his voice,
but now I look like shit.
And I feel sick.

What the fuck are you doing here?

JIM I wanted to check in on you. Last time I came you were –

JESSIE You've been up before?

JIM A few times.

JESSIE Right. I thought you may have. I just... Didn't know if it were...

JIM That's why I had to keep coming back.

JESSIE Oh that's why is it?

JIM Didn't want you thinking you'd made me up.

JESSIE Well, now I know I haven't.

JIM Best be off then.

JESSIE Shut up.

JIM I'm joking.

JESSIE I know, you dickhead.

JIM I wouldn't know where to go anyway... we got kicked out of Unit 2.

JESSIE How come?

JIM Repossession. It was a guardianship so was bound to happen at some point.

JESSIE What about Allie?

And I suddenly question if...

But Jim immediately spots it and says quick.

JIM She's fine.

Beat.

So...what is it then?

JESSIE Nothing.

JIM Go on.

JESSIE It's...a painting.

JIM Let's see.

JESSIE No.

JIM Go on, you said you're a painter. Let me see how good you are.

> **JESSIE** *gives him the paper.*

Not bad.

JESSIE I did it when I was like eight.

JIM Are your parents dressed as...

JESSIE Superheroes. Yeah.

JIM Your mum looks pretty sick.

JESSIE Wonder Woman.

JIM Who are you meant to be?

JESSIE Frenchy from *Grease* I think.

JIM I think you should put it back up. Looked good.

> *He gives it back.*

JESSIE Yeah. Maybe.

> *Pause.*

JIM I should probably head off. Nice to see you. It's good to know you're... Don't be a stranger.

> **JIM** *goes to leave.*

JESSIE Stay with us? For a bit. Please?

JIM Course. Whatever you need.

JESSIE And he does. Up until now, actually.

We head downstairs to see Donna and Paul
and over the next few months we all
sort out dad's estate
and as we do I feel a weight
lift from off of me. We repaint
and the house feels completely different.
It feels like a new place.
A place that I could live in.
Ralph comes back from Norway
and all he has to say is –

RALPH Norway's fuckin' shit mate.

JESSIE Before he helps redecorate the kitchen.

We get some exciting news from Allie too.
She's on the radio on that station
where they introduce people who are new.
She doesn't tell us when though.
So we have it on a lot just in case
it's her slot to play and when it is
it fucking makes my day.

> **ALLIE**
> I'M PUTTING ON MY HIGH
> WAISTED JEANS
> THE FIRST TIME IN DECADES IT
> SEEMS
> AS I STARE AT THIS ROOM
> FILLED WITH MEMORIES
> AND MY ARMY OF STARDUST
> AND DREAMS
> AND MUCH MORE THAN ONCE IN
> A WHILE
> I THINK OF YOU THINK OF YOUR
> SMILE

> THINK OF THE WAY THAT
> THINGS USED TO BE
> FOREVER BE MISSING YOUR
> COMPANY

I stopped the psych meds.
But I still see someone once a week.
Mostly the voices have stopped
but definitely not
completely.

> **ALLIE**
> BLUE IS HIS FAVOURITE AND I
> THINK
> I STILL HEAR HIS VOICE AND
> THEN I BLINK
> I MISS SEEING DISHES BY THE
> SINK
> I STILL HAVE THE RUM HE USED
> TO DRINK

They come back every now and again
when I'm feeling run down.
Or hungover or I'm shattered.
It's usually then,
when they poke their ugly noses in.
But I've learnt to live with them.

> **ALLIE**
> EACH DAY IS ANOTHER LITTLE
> STEP
> I THINK OF THE LESSONS THAT
> HE LEFT
> WHENEVER I'M FEELING SO
> BEREFT
> I THINK OF HIS VOICE WITH
> EVERY BREATH

And I couldn't have done it without my friends.

So I want to raise a glass and make a toast

to the two most important people in my life.

Thank you for helping me through
the most difficult time I've ever faced.
There's really nothing left I can say

You two are perfect for each other
from party animals, to lovers and now soul mates.
I wish you the best in all that life sends your way.

I love you. Thank you.

RALPH That is so fucking lame.

JESSIE Why you such a dickhead, Ralph?

To the happy couple.

(The whole room drinks.)

I look at you all and once again I think:

We are made of stardust and dreams.

All that's actually there, is you and me.
And I won't waste this once in a trillion opportunity.
I will be there for you,
just as you have been there for me.

End

SET AND PROPS

Set:
The set should be made up of the instruments the performers use.
The aesthetic of the show should be in keeping with the conventions of a gig.
Any excess set should also be in keeping with these conventions, e.g. speakers for seats, etc.

Props:
1 × Water painting of Jessie and her parents.
1 × Rucksack which Paul brings in at the end of the housewarming.

Equipment used in the original production:

1 × acoustic drum kit
2 × guitar
1 × bass guitar
1 × keyboard
1 × saxophone
1 × electric violin
1 × BOSS effects pedal
1 × UltraNova Synth
1 × AKAI MPC Live
2 × Korg Kaoss pads (KP3)
1 × handheld radio microphone
5 × dynamic vocal microphones
1 × dynamic vocal microphone run through effects moderator (KP3)
1 × Haze Machine
3 × large speakers

A million wires.

VISIT THE
SAMUEL FRENCH
BOOKSHOP
AT THE
ROYAL COURT THEATRE

Browse plays and theatre books, get expert advice and enjoy a coffee

Samuel French Bookshop
Royal Court Theatre
Sloane Square
London
SW1W 8AS
020 7565 5024

Shop from thousands of titles on our website

 samuelfrench.co.uk

 samuelfrenchltd

 samuel french uk